AF365577

CUENTOS, POEMAS Y FRASES ÚTILES
PARA IMPARTIR UNA ASIGNATURA EN INGLÉS
(TERCER CICLO DE PRIMARIA)

TITETA IS A PART OF MY FAMILY (introduce yourself, to be, present simple, present continuous).

I WANT TO BE A MUSICIAN (present simple to be, present continuous, jobs, subjects and musical instruments).

MUM'S WARDROBE (descriptions, comparative and superlative).

A PINK CHICK (Easter, present simple and present continuous).

I WANT TO BE A BULLFIGHTER! (wh- questions, opinion, jobs, plans, "want to be").

A VEGETARIAN DILOPHOSAURIUS (health and Earth Day, like + gerund, want to + inf.).

FOLLOW THE RULES (descriptions, to be in past, imperative, past simple).
PUNK (descriptions, there was / were, past simple).

A GIRAFFE WITHOUT SPOTS (descriptions, plans: going to, Christmas, town and city).

THE MAGIC GOAT (town, city, transport and street).

THE TELESCOPE WANTS TO BE ORIGINAL (journeys, Valentine's Day).

USEFUL LANGUAGE FOR THE CLASSROOM

Copyright © Pilar Bellés Pitarch, 2014
1ª edición: agosto 2014
ISBN:978-84-617-1351-6
Depósito Legal: CS-274-2014

Pilar Bellés Pitarch (1964) es licenciada en Filología Inglesa y profesora de inglés. Hace años que se dedica a investigar sobre las posibilidades del cuento para desarrollar la creatividad y trabajar valores. También cuenta con investigaciones sobre métodos para aprender inglés.

Estos son los cuentos y poesías que usa en sus clases de inglés. Cada cuento tiene sus imágenes en color y su poema. A los niños de esta edad les gusta recitar poemas en lengua extranjera y así, mientras escuchan el cuento en inglés interactúan y usan la lengua.

Son de gran utilidad tanto para los profesores o profesoras de inglés como para los padres y madres que quieran mejorar el nivel de inglés de sus hijos o hijas.

Pilar Bellés cuenta además con numerosas publicaciones en cuento, novela y poesía.

Publicaciones sobre cuentos plurilingües y valores en el campo de la enseñanza:

•"Telling a tale / Contemos un cuento / Contem un conte" (adaptados a los centros de interés de educación infantil).

• "Cuentos plurilingües para trabajar valores y para días especiales" (día del árbol, día de la paz, Halloween…)

•"¿Cómo hacer alumnos creativos?" (cuentos plurilingües para desarrollar la creatividad y, a la vez, trabajar valores para todas las edades).

• "No dejes que crezca sin la magia de los cuentos… según lo que quieras transmitir, elige un cuento y… cuéntaselo" (alternativa a los cuentos tradicionales).

Métodos para aprender inglés a través de la literatura:

•"Els iaios, la natura i l'amor / Los abuelos, la naturaleza y el amor / Grandparents, Love and Nature" (método de las historias plurilingües).

•"Federico y su duende / Frederick and his Goblin" (método de las historias bilingües).

Novela:

•"El diario mágico" (contra la violencia de género). Ediciones Carena.

•"Somos víctimas de una sociedad machista y cruel" (contra el machismo y la desigualdad). Ediciones Grup Lobher.

•"El mensaje" (contra el acoso y la manipulación). Ediciones Carena.

•"La rosa deshojada" (contra la violencia de género) de Pilar Bellés y Maribel Rueda. JNQ Ediciones.

•"Triunfar en tiempos difíciles" con el método de los relatos interrelacionados. JNQ Ediciones.

."Reunión de colegas" (se nos manipula sin que nos demos cuenta…). Editorial Lulu.

Biografía:
. "Toda una vida: memorias y anécdotas de Mel y Xispa". De Manuel Falcó García (Xispa) y Pilar Bellés Pitarch. Editorial viveLibro.

. Teatro: "Engaño perfecto". Editorial Lulu.

. Poesía: "Curvas en el camino". Ediciones Carena.

. Ensayo: "Educar en valores actuales a través de la literatura y otros ensayos". Editorial Lulu.

TITETA IS A PART OF MY FAMILY

(introduce yourself, to be, present simple, present continuous)

'This is my pet, she is a budgie,' says Miguel.
''What's her name?' ask his friends.
'She is Titeta.'
'How old is she?'
'She is three years old.'
She is special because she is a part of my family. This is her story.
'Dad didn't like hairy animals because they made a mess of his house. But Mum wanted a pet for me and I wanted an animal. Finally, they bought a pair of budgies, Tito and Tita. Tito was green and Tita was blue.'
Miguel and Mum taught their budgies to talk, but budgies didn't talk. They kissed one another and played together, but those budgies didn't like people. It was a bad experience for Miguel and Mum.
'You can't caress a budgie like a dog. It's impossible,' says Dad.
'I want a dog,' says Miguel.
'Noooooooooo!' says Mum.

I've got two budgies
Green and blue,
They caress and kiss
But they don't talk to you,
I wanted a dog
Noooooo!

Months later Tita dies. Tito is sad. It is Miguel's birthday and his parents give him a present: Tita II.
'But… I wanted a dog.'
'Noooooooo!'
When they put Tita II into her cage, Tito isn't there. He has escaped.
'What can we do with this animal?' says Mum.
'Whatever you want…' says Miguel.
'Wait! I've got an idea,' says Dad.
He picks up Tita II in his hands and… What a surprise! He can pick up the bird.
'Dad is picking up Titeta,' says Miguel.
'Let's fly,' says Dad.
Tita II flies through the living room happily… She has got beautiful feathers.
'She is beautiful…' says Mum.
'Titeta is flying!' shouts Miguel.
 'It's only a baby…' says Dad.

Tita dies
Tito goes away,
It's Miguel's birthday
Titeta is flying,
Miguel says.

ç

Unhappily Titeta breaks her leg. They take her to the vet, they look after her and they feed her.

'We are looking after Titeta,' says Miguel.

A month later, Titeta is like a baby for them. They can pick her up. Miguel plays with her. He chases her through the house and the garage.

'I'm playing with Titeta. Titeta is flying. I'm chasing her.'

Dad and Mum love Titeta too. Titeta rides on Mum's shoulder most of the time.

'Titeta is riding on Mum's shoulder.'

Titeta only goes to her cage to eat and to the toilet. When there is a party Titeta is the centre of attention.   Titeta likes going out of the house on Mum's shoulder, she doesn't fly away. She is happy at home with Mum, Dad and brother.

Titeta is a baby,
She is flying
But she doesn't fly away,
And playing with me
Most of the time.

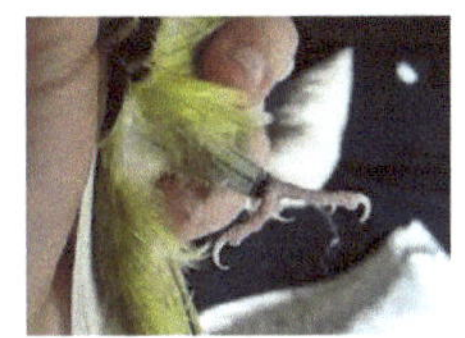
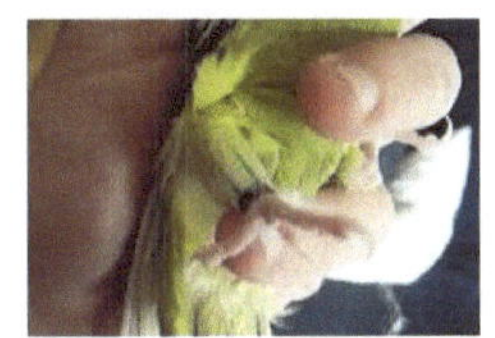

One day Miguel, Dad and Mum take Titeta by car to visit Miguel's grandmother.
'We are visiting my granny.'
'What a nice animal!' says Granny.
Then they go back to their car. Miguel is so happy that he turns on the radio.
Titeta gets scared and she flies and flies. She is lost.
 What have you done?' asks Mum. She is angry.
'I don't know…Titeta is lost…' says Miguel crying.
They didn't know what to do.
'Let's go and look for her!' says Dad.
Miguel, Dad and Mum run in the same direction Titeta flew.
She is on a car windscreen waiting for them. She is scared.
Dad calls her name and she flies to his shoulder. Miguel and Mum kiss her and they go home.
Now they know Titeta is a part of their family. Persistence and effort are necessary to get our purposes. Titeta got it. But we must be careful with limitations.

Titeta goes by car
To visit granny
Don't fly away
Stay here
With your family.

TITETA IS A PART OF MY FAMILY

I've got two budgies
Green and blue,
They caress and kiss
But they don't talk to you,
I wanted a dog
Noooooo!

Tita dies
Tito goes away,
It's Miguel's birthday
Titeta is flying,
Miguel says.

Titeta is a baby,
She is flying
But she doesn't fly away,
And playing with me
Most of the time.

Titeta goes by car
To visit granny,
Don't fly away,
Stay here
With your family.

INTRODUCE YOURSELF: USEFUL LANGUAGE

Introduce yourself: Hello! I'm (...); what's your name?; his/her name's (...); I like your (...); how old are you?; I'm (ten); have you got (any brothers or sisters)?; I've got (...); I haven't got (...); animals. It's good to hear you. Let's all meet again. How old is he/she? What's his/her name? My/His / Her name is (...). Has he/she got a brother/sister? Where does he/she live? I like playing (the drums/English).He/She likes (playing guitar). She's good at (singing). I've/She's got a (...). He / She hasn't got a (...)? I have/No I haven't. Where/What does he sleep/eat? He sleeps (...)/eats (...).

Vocabulary: days of the week, objects of the classroom, the alphabet; age, family, food, everybody, great, rollerblades, twins, tennis racket, wardrobe, basket, summer camp, furniture, routines, animals and food; Open Day; welcome; days of the week, months and subjects; classroom; armchair, sock and shoe.

Sentences: where's/re my (pen/s)? Have got (objects / family); new; excuse me; here you are; please; sorry; thank you; thanks; my favourite (...) is (...); both. Hip, hip, hurray! This is (...).That's right. This is a (...). It's for (...). Something to (...). Beginning with (...). I love (...). (It) was. Sorry! Is it behind/in/on/under the table / door. Yes it is/No it isn't.

PRESENT SIMPLE AND PRESENT CONTINUOUS: USEFUL LANGUAGE

Verbs: Present Simple, Present Continuous. Past simple of verb to be; can; throw.

Vocabulary: dragon; knight/s; hero/es; kite; scared; parts of the body; legend; programme; kinds of stories (animal, adventure, true, funny); telling the time; plural of substantives; days of the week; hydra; cage; cave; comparatives; heroine; queen; Egypt; Greece; adjectives; animals; food, free time activities, sports, health, months of the year, ancient; message; crying; happy; laughing; sad;

colours; the alphabet; action verbs; snorkelling; climbing; flying a kite; badminton; basketball; disco dancing; fantastic; fixing (things); language; machine; bright; here; too; very; hero / heroine; really; all; universe;   hall;   rock; cover; places; title; fight; sword; the bottom; coin; heads; tails; faces; faraway; handsome; arrows; art gallery, deer; lions; long ago; museum; painting; peasant: dream; love; piece (of cheese); everyday things; people to know; ; times long ago.

Sentences: do you like (adventure stories)? Yes, I do /No, I don't; there is/are; where was he from? has got; is good at; what's your favourite (...)?; where are you?; what are you doing?; I like/I don't like; free time activities and hobbies; what are you good at?; I'm good at (...);what you do/don't you like doing?; what about (...)?;listening to music; yes, I do/no, I don't; tickets; have you got (...)?; do you like (...)?; are/is (...)?; do you want to come? It doesn't work. Milo pushes the light. This is the wall. I can hear a voice. I've got a medal. I'm an artist. I think (...) is fantastic; breaking the door. Life was hard.

Computer vocabulary: browse; click; download; keyboard; Internet;   mouse;   screen;   scroll   down;   magazine; newspaper; webpage; website.

I WANT TO BE A MUSICIAN

(present simple to be, present continuous, jobs, subjects
and musical instruments)

David, a rich man, had got a budgie. They are talking:
'What's your name?' asks David.
'My name is Eth.' says the budgie.
'Where do you live?'
'I live in a big and comfortable house.'
'What's your favourite subject?'
'I like Music.'
'What do you want to be?'
'I want to be an authentic rock musician.'
'You are too small and instruments are too big. We haven't
got a band and we haven't got instruments. It's impossible.'

Eth is a budgie,
He can talk,
He likes Music
But he is too small.

One day Eth flies away. He wants to make his dreams a reality.
He can fly but he doesn't know the way. He asks the way and he travels by bus, by train, by car, by bike, on foot…
By luck he finds other budgies that want to be rock musicians. There are other budgies with the same dream.
They find a music school to study. But, where are the instruments? They get in unobserved. It is a bi
g orchestra. Instruments are too big and they can't move them or play them. It is impossible.

Eth flies away
To make his dreams reality
He doesn't know the way
To have an opportunity.

Eth returns home. He is very sad and disappointed. David is waiting for him and he smiles but Eth is very sad.
One day Eth pecks rhythmically on wood. It is a beautiful melody. Then other and another one David listens to him.
David takes Eth to the rock school and he orders to make small instruments for Eth and his friends.
They were the first band of rock musician budgies in the word. They were very successful.
Finally, his dream was real.

David orders to make
Small instruments
For Eth and his friends,
Eth can play
In a big band
And their dream was real,
They are happy
One, two, three.

Microphone
Record
Accordion
Bugle
Drum
Flute
Guitar
Harmonica
Harp
Keyboard
Piano
Saxophone
by plane
by car
by train
by bike
by bus
by boat
on foot

I WANT TO BE A MUSICIAN

Eth is a budgie,
He can talk,
He likes Music
But he is too small.

Eth flies away
To make his dreams reality
He doesn't know the way
To have an opportunity.

David orders to make
Small instruments
For Eth and his friends,
Eth can play
In a big band
And their dream was real;
They are happy
One, two, three.

SUBJECTS, DAYS OF THE WEEK, MONTHS: USEFUL LANGUAGE

Subjects, days and time: We have (Maths) on (Monday) at (3 o'clock); a quarter past/to; Art; Computer Studies; English; Geography; History; Maths; Music; Science; Sport; my favourite subject is (...); What time do you (...)?; Africa;;
Vocabulary: timetable; days of the week, the time, friends; in the (morning); classroom; corridor; dining room; field; games; songs. Hurry!; marathon; quick; floors; ship; socks; hairy; scary; smiles; canoes; count: every day; history.
Verbs: clean; get dressed; wake up; Present Simple; routines, get the bus; dreams; go to bed; have breakfast; clean my teeth; comb my hair; look in the mirror; learn, walk; the bottom of the ship.
Sentences: Let's go; there's; we have; I need (...); It's late. It's dark. Go away! Wait! Make things. Remember things.

ANIMALS / FOOD / COUNTRIES: USEFUL LANGUAGE

Animals: bison; chimpanzee; hippo; owl; parrot; zebra; brown bears; giant pandas; polar bears.
Food: berries, bamboo shoots; leaves, plants;
Sentences, wh- questions: What do they eat? They eat… Where are they from? they are from… Where do they live? They live in… They can (can/have got/are...); fly; jump; swing; angry.
Continents and countries: Africa; America; Poland; China
Places: cave; den; nest.
Bugs: ant; bee; beetle; bug; files; grasshopper; fly.

MUM'S WARDROBE
(descriptions, comparative and superlative)

Mum loves her wardrobe. Each morning she looks at her nice costumes, suits, dresses, trousers, sweaters, clothes, skirts, shirts, jackets, belts, shoes… and she smiles.

'Good morning, lovely woman,' says the wardrobe.

'Good morning, dear!' says she. 'What can I wear today? I want a shorter skirt. This dress is the most beautiful in the world.'

'Let's see… How do you feel today?'

The wardrobe loves Mum because she puts rich treasures there.

She looks at herself in the mirror, she closes her eyes and, suddenly, she thinks what she would like to wear today.

Mum's wardrobe

Is magic

She looks her clothes

And closes her eyes.

Mum and the wardrobe are happy together. Dad and the boy are jealous:
'You are always talking to the wardrobe' says Dad. 'Are you married with the wardrobe? It's enough!'
Mum likes shopping. The wardrobe is always full. It is too full. It falls down and it is broken in two halves. Mum is crying.
'What am I going to do without my wardrobe? It's magic...'
First Dad and the boy celebrate. But then they get worried. Mum is sad. She doesn't tidy herself.

The wardrobe is broken
What has happened?
It was magic
Now there isn't.

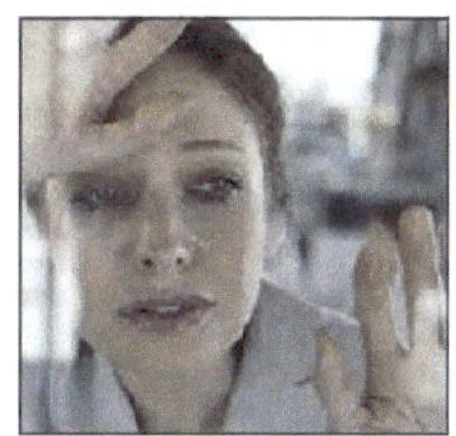

Once Mum is arriving at home.

'Surprise!' shouts Dad and the boy together. 'Close your eyes and go to your bedroom. You can open your eyes.'

'Wow! My wardrobe! You have it repaired! I've all my clothes in my wardrobe. But it is bigger than before!'

'We added a supplement. You need more space and your happiness is important for us.'

'But it's more expensive than a new wardrobe… Wow! It's the biggest wardrobe in the world!'

'It's not important… It's for you.'

Mum takes Dad and her son in her arms before looking at herself in the wardrobe mirror.

After that, when she gets up she smiles at her family and she talks to them. She'll never talk to the wardrobe again. She's got a nice family.

The wardrobe again
With a supplement,
I love my family
We are happy,
One, two, three.

MUM'S WARDROBE

Mum's wardrobe
Is magic
She looks her clothes
And closes her eyes.

The wardrobe is broken
What has happened?
It was magic
Now there isn't.

The wardrobe again
With a supplement,
I love my family
We are happy,
One, two, three.

DESCRIPTIONS / COMPARATIVE AND SUPERLATIVE: USEFUL LANGUAGE

Adjectives: fat; thin; dark; fair; huge; short; tall; cold; hot; old; young; good looking; ugly; long; straight; curly; dark; fair; loud; beautiful;

Comparative and superlative: is (her sister) younger than (my sister)?; yes, she is; no, she isn't; (...);(...) is (...) than (...); the same as; is (...) (...) than (...)?; cheapest; more expensive; smallest; biggest; good; better; best; slowest; fastest; bad; worse; worst.

Vocabulary: rat; tail; birthday; celebrate; illness; days of the week; months of the year; parts of the body; animals and parts of their body; llama; circle; line; same; smile; trousers; members of the family; cool! Invitation, show, emperor, face; around, down; magician, illusion; together, glasses; flute; piano; coffee; drum; violin; pop; rock; classical; guitarist; suitcase; prize; Broadway; front; musical; show (n); theatre, CD, guitar, ticket, t-shirt; monument, mountain, ocean, river, Oklahoma; the sound of music; the ground floor. XL (Extra Large), window, Hawaii, outside, youth festival.

Sentences: when's your birthday?; it's in… I can't wait. Right? Yuck! We're strong and fit. What are you talking about? Guess who. I know. Our eyes are playing tricks on our brains. What's happening? How much? Which?

Verbs: belongs to; relax; dance; study; explore; compose; Present Continuous. Past Simple. Can, break, maybe, put on (a musical), take, move, remember.

A PINK CHICK
(Easter, present simple and present continuous)

It's Easter time. There are Easter chicks everywhere. There is a place where blue is a colour for boys and pink is for girls. A pink chick is born.
'What can we do?' says Mum.
'This is unacceptable' shouts Dad. 'Pink is for girls…'
'Why?' says the brother.
'No, no, no… This is unacceptable.'
People are sad and worried.

Blue for boys
Pink for girls
This boy is pink,
One, two, three.

Blue boys

Pink girls

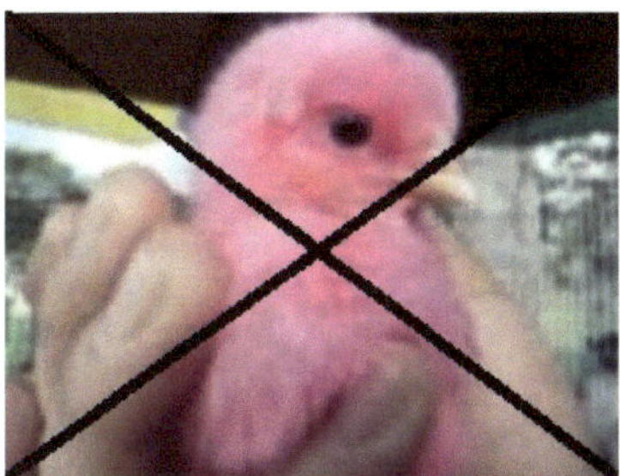

A pink boy?

A group of foreign chicks arrives. They are different: girls are yellow and boys are pink.
Finally the pink chick finds other pink chicks.
People are not sad or worried and they celebrate Easter.
Different Easter chicks are playing together and they are friends. It doesn't matter their colour. It is nonsense.
This is the end of the story.

Now girls are yellow
And boys are pink
Pink, yellow or blue,
Boys or girls
It doesn't mean
Anything…

Pink boys   Yellow girls

A PINK CHICK

Blue for boys
Pink for girls
This boy is pink,
One, two, three.

Now girls are yellow
And boys are pink
Pink, yellow or blue,
Boys or girls
It doesn't mean
Anything…

EASTER: USEFUL LANGUAGE

Vocabulary: champion; chicks; Easter; eggs; first; last; paint; American; behind; between; chocolate; garden; grass; many; stay; tree; colours; months of the year; kitten; lamb; piglet; puppy; fingerprints; need; pond; basket; field; football; sweets; animals; classroom objects; colours; cross the line; Easter Egg Roll; icing sugar; shape; symbol; huge; pond.

I WANT TO BE A BULLFIGHTER!
(wh- questions, opinion, jobs, plans, "want to be")

It is the feast of the patron in the town. There are bulls in the square. Children play bulls.
A boy asks for a bull from his mother:
'Do you like bulls, Mum?'
'Yes, I do,' says Mum.
'Where do they live?'
'They live in the country.'
'What do they eat?'
'They eat grass.'
'Where do they sleep?
'They sleep in a bull yard.'
'Where are they from?'
'They are from Valencia.'
'Mum, I want to have a bull for my birthday and a bull game for my console,' says he.
'OK,' says Mum.
They go to the fair. Mum buys a plastic bull. The bull's skin is similar to hair.

I like bulls
In the bull yard,
Yes, I do.
Bulls in the square.

At home the small boy plays with the plastic bull. In the street he plays bulls with other children. In the square the barriers are ready.

'What do you want to be?' says Mum.

'I want to be a bullfighter,' says the boy.

Finally, the first day of bulls begins.

People wear shorts and T-shirts. People go to their scaffold with the group of friends. For the small boy it was a long afternoon. The bull runs in the square. People infuriate it and avoid it. In their scaffolds, other children are too big to play with him. He is sitting on a corner and he is playing with his plastic bull.

'What do you want to be?'
The first day of bulls begins,
At scaffolds with friends,
Watch the bulls and play.

It is break time. The small boy says Mum:
'I want to fight a bull, Mum.'
They go to the bull yard. There is a barrier around the yard.
They can see the bulls next to them.
'I like the bigger one. The black one,' says the boy.
'Oh! It's the bull,' says Mum. 'The others are cows. They are
less strong than the bull. It's the last one in the square
before the break time.'
'Yes, I want to be a bullfighter.'
Suddenly some bigger boys make a strong noise next to
them. The big black bull runs against the barrier where they
are. There is an impact. The barrier is moving.
People get scared. The boy and his mum go away to their
scaffold.

Bulls are dangerous,
The boy says,
Barriers are moving,
Let's go away.

Luckily barriers are safe and everything is all right. Now, they are on their scaffold.

'I don't want to be a bullfighter. They are too dangerous,' says the boy.

'Yes, they are,' says a woman who sits next to him.

'Fighting bulls in the square is a barbarity!' says a man.

Yes. But bulls and orchestra are the only attractions we have in festivals. If we don't have bulls, what can we do during our festivities?'

'No idea…'

'What do you think?'

Bulls or no bulls,
This is the question,
What do you think?
Give me your opinion
One, two, three.

bulls   no bulls

I WANT TO BE A BULLFIGHTER!

I like bulls
In the bull yard,
Yes, I do.
Bulls in the square.

'What do you want to be?'
The first day of bulls begins,
At scaffolds with friends,
Watch the bulls and play.

Bulls are dangerous,
The boy says,
Barriers are moving,
Let's go away.

Bulls or no bulls,
This is the question,
What do you think?
Give me your opinion
One, two, three.

JOBS / PRESENT TO BE / WANT TO: USEFUL LANGUAGE

Jobs: cleaner; cook; dancer; dentist; photographer; pilot; reporter; singer; secretary; train driver.

Countries: Brazil; China; Ecuador; Spain; Italy; England; Great Britain; France; American; Brazilian; Chinese; English; French; Italian; Spanish.

Verbs: I want; he/she wants to be a (...); travel; present simple, 3rd person singular.

Vocabulary: film; uniform; the world; old languages; rocks; soil; study; mechanic; geologist; kitchen; an office; wonderful; guitar; night; paper; phone; shower; window; ambulance driver; flag; Red Cross; town; vet; village; never mind, smile, neighbours, city museum, collection, name, real, suddenly, team, hospital, night, people, school, weekends, lonely, mistery, crisis, emergency, organization.

Sentences: he/she's from (...). What does he/she do? He/she's a (...). Be careful. Yes, of course. Where's he from? All alone.

BIRTHDAY

Verbs: blow; invite, make a wish, cover, enjoy a treat.

Vocabulary: candle; present; special; balloon; bingo; invitation; moths of the year, festivals, bag, coloured sweets, jar of chocolate spread, packet.

A VEGETARIAN DILOPHOSAURIUS
(health and Earth Day, like + gerund, want to + inf.)

A dilophosaurus decides to eat only vegetables. He doesn't like killing other animals to eat.
'I don't like meat because I don't like killing other animals.'
His family doesn't like his decision. He has got lots of problems.
'I don't want to eat meat. From now on, I'm going to eat vegetables.'
'No, you aren't, says the others.

I don't want meat,
No, I don't,
From now on,
I'm going to eat
Vegetables.

Other dinosaurs don't respect his option and they make jokes about it. His family is ashamed of him because he eats vegetables.

'Let's do a competition,' says his older brother. 'We'll run around the island for an hour. The winner decides. If I'm the winner you'll eat meat and if you're the winner I'll eat vegetables.'

 'I don't like competitions, and I don't like fighting with my brother. I'm going to another island to live.'

They don't respect my option,
And make jokes
About it.
I don't like competitions,
And I'm going to another island
To live.

Meanwhile there is a volcanic explosion and all the carnivorous dinosaurs die. He doesn't die.

After the explosion, he comes back to see his family. There is nothing. Everything is burned.

He walks and walks and he find an injured female dilophosaur. She has got a broken leg. He cures her and he gives her vegetables to eat. They plant more trees and save their planet.

Sometime later the female dilophosaurus is herbivorous too. They are married and they have three children.

"What are their names?"

"The oldest boy is Centurion, the medium one is Medium and the youngest one is a girl called Purpurine".

From then on, the dilophosarus eat vegetables for a long time. Unhappily they disappeared.

They save the planet
They plant more trees
They have got three children
Centurion, Medium
And Purpurine.
All they are vegetarian
One, two, three.

A VEGETARIAN DILOPHOSAUR

I don't want meat
No, I don't
From now on,
I'm going to eat
Vegetables.

They don't respect my option,
And make jokes
About it.
I don't like competitions,
And I'm going to another island
To live.

They save the planet
They plant more trees
They have got three children
Centurion, Medium
And Purpurine.
All they are vegetarian
One, two, three.

HEALTH: USEFUL LANGUAGE

Sentences: What's the matter?; I've got a (cold / cough / headhache / sore throat / flu); I'm not very well; he's got a broken (...);; I can see (...); I'm red and hot. All day. Oh, dear! Follow me. Can you help me? Yes, of course. Yes, sure.

Verbs: imperatives; have got; can/can't; get well; there's/there're; celebrate; want; come; give a drink.

Vocabulary: earache; toothache; I'm better; baby; doctor; grandad; parts of the body; children; feet; teeth; drink; idea; sheep; a/an; lemon; honey; aliments; healthy; vet; wing, clown; funny; ill; joke; laughing; picnic; illness; nurse; except; every, roar, worried, box, down. Wow!; hospital, patients.

EARTH DAY: USEFUL LANGUAGE

Sentences: clean the water; Earth Day; plant more trees; recycle; save our planet; build bird houses; organise a nature walk; pick up rubbish; turn off the lights; please save.

Verbs: throw; wash; celebrate; help; let's; join; plant; save; want to.

Vocabulary: bin; a cake stall; cup; glass; bottle; by bike; planet; trees; earth-friendly.

FOLLOW THE RULES

(descritions, to be in past, imperative, past simple)

There was a boy called Miguel. He was eleven. When he rode his bike Mum said:
'Wear your helmet, be careful on the road, don't sit on the handlebars, don't stand on the seat, your feet must touch the pedals.' But specially: 'Don't pedal on the other side. It's too dangerous.'
Miguel likes the road. When he rode down he pedals on the other side to slow down. He didn't use the brakes.
He liked the fresh air on his face. It was great!

Riding on your bike,
Pedalling on the other side,
Descending quickly,
The fresh air on his face,
It was great.

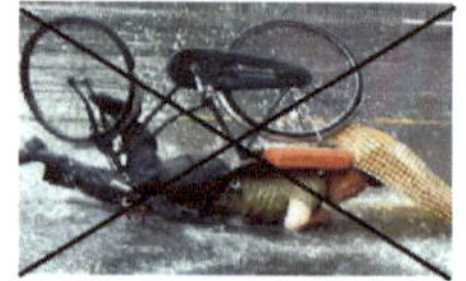

Once while he was descending and pedalling in the other side, a pedal fell off. The bike was out of control and Miguel fell down.
When Miguel arrived home he was crying. He has got a big lump on his head. He was injured. His bike was broken.

A pedal fell off
Pedalling on the other side,
His bike was broken,
And he was crying.

They went to the doctor. Luckily, it was nothing but Miguel had got a big ball on his head for a week and a big headache.
For this reason there are rules. Miguel always follows the rules. Do you?

Luckily
It was nothing,
He was sick
For a week,
Now he follows the rules,
Do you?

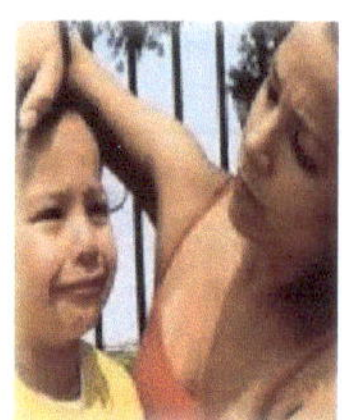
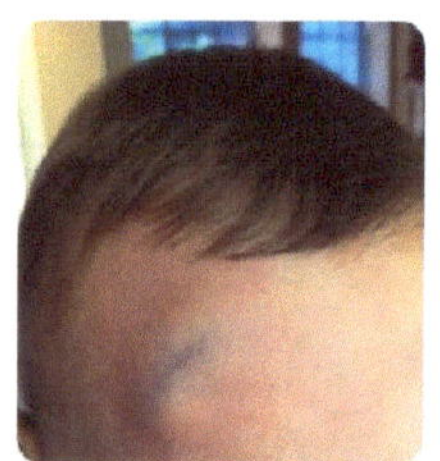

FOLLOW THE RULES

Riding on your bike,
Pedalling on the other side,
Descending quickly,
The fresh air on his face,
It was great.

A pedal fell off
Pedalling on the other side,
His bike was broken,
And he was crying.

Luckily
It was nothing,
He was sick
For a week,
Now he follows the rules,
Do you?

WAS, WERE / DESCRIPTIONS: USEFUL LANGUAGE

Verbs: past simple of to be.
Vocabulary: claws; a vegetarian; comparative adjectives, appearance, parts of the body , sharp; numbers 1-100; friendly; scared; behind; forest; across; between; down; through; up; on; in; teddy; yesterday; peaceful; planet; spots; webbed; stairs, well; puppy; brain.
Sentences: How long was its body/were its claws? It was (...) metres long. How tall was it? How do you know that? Do you know this dinosaur? Follow the footsteps.

FOOD / IMPERATIVE: USEFUL LANGUAGE

Verbs: imperatives, present simple.
Food: mussels; oil; prawns; pepper; rice; red pepper; salt; vinegar; cereal; cheese; eggs; fruit; milk; tea; toast; yoghurt; black olives; boiled eggs; cooked potatoes; fizzy drink; mayonnaise; onion; peas; tomato; vegetables; across.
Vocabulary: fridge box; jug; pan; spoon; healthy; bug; first; later; llama; menu; next; palace; pie; restaurant; then; waitress; wife; add; cut; dish; mix; spoonful; strips; finally; diagonally; square; never mind; alarm clock; butter; clean your teeth; flavour; plum; biscuits; lettuce; score card; a criss-cross pattern; a treat; bedroom; kitchen; early; stretch; vegetarian; summer; winter; chocolate; ice; lemon; strawberry; adults; a long time; calcium; dessert; idea; metal bowl; protein; vitamin; special meal of the day.
Sentences: relax for a time. Call the waitress on the table. I've got an idea. Count the ticks. Go round three times. Put a counter on start. Throw the dice. Eat/sleep.

PUNK

(descriptions, there was / were, past simple)

Once upon a time there was a boy with punk hair.
Time before he had arrived at school with punk hair and he had said that words:
'You must call me Punk.'
He thought nobody remembered his real name or his previous appearance.
 At school everybody followed the game and they called him Punk.

I've got punk hair,
Call me Punk,
Everybody follows the game
At school.

One morning he hasn't got hair cream. There is no hair cream in the shop and he can't use it. His hair is curly.
'There was no hair cream in the shop. It's finished,' says Mum. 'I couldn't buy it.'
'Oh no! Today my hair is not punk. What can I do? Everybody knows Punk, the important boy. Nobody remembers Joseph, the ordinary boy…'

Today there is no hair cream
My hair isn't punk
Now my hair is curly
It's a problem for me.

His friends remember Joseph and they like him.
'Hello Joseph. I like your new hair,' says one friend.
'Today I am an ordinary boy.'
'You aren't ordinary, you are special for us. You are our friend. You can have straight hair, curly hair, long hair, short hair or punk hair. Your hair doesn't matter. You are our friend.'
'Finally you have the right option. Your punk hair is horrible…' says another friend.
Punk disappeared and Joseph appeared. His friends accepted him. His physical aspect didn't matter.
And this was the end of the story.

Your hair doesn't matter:
Straight, curly, long,
Short, dark and blond.
You are our friend
And this is the end;
We are happy
One, two, three.

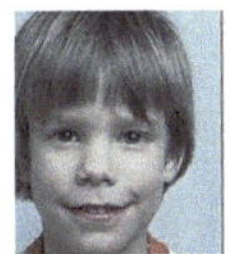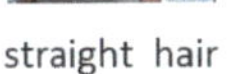    

straight hair   curly hair   blonde hair   black hair   punk hair

PUNK

I've got punk hair,
Call me Punk,
Everybody follows the game
At school.

Today there is no hair cream
My hair isn't punk
Now my hair is curly
It's a problem for me.

Your hair doesn't matter:
Straight, curly, long,
Short, dark and blond.
You are our friend
And this is the end;
We are happy
One, two, three.

straight hair   curly hair   blonde hair   black hair   punk hair

THERE WAS / THERE WERE: USEFUL LANGUAGE

Verbs: There was/were; past simple to be and regular verbs; erupt; present continuous; sail; build; change (v); conserve.
Prepositions: on/in/into; jump in/into; stand next to.
Vocabulary: pets' corner; playground; pond; see-saw; slide; swings; in 2001; hot; cold; rain; wind; a drought; a freeze; a flood; a hurricane; cloudy; dry; sunny; wet; windy; fireball; island; lake; the sea; the valley; crash into; destroy; sorry; alive; ash; thunderbolts; lucky; noise; scared; storm; strange; terrible; volcano; AD; August 24th; boats; fun; goat; horrid; hungry; the oceans; pelican; plants; sailor; the Eden Project; empty (v); greenhouse; machines; medicine; plants; plural nouns; park; shopping; pets; cities; forest; horses; Internet cafés; shops; days of the week; seasons; adjectives; dinosaur; lemur; diary; Italy; Naples; eggs; the land; rat; the sky; tortoise; lonesome; a future; a past; long ago; more and more; the last of my family; dates; planet; an enormous hole; Ever again; Impossible to work.
Sentences: (that) wasn't; do you remember (...)? Remember? What a shame! Everything is changing. Life (is good). Watch out. Live our lives the way they were before?

PAST SIMPLE: USEFUL LANGUAGE

Verbs: fly, flew; sail, sailed; erupt, erupted; rain, rained; change, changed; invent, invented, pull, pulled; change, changed the world.
Vocabulary: aeroplane; engine; kite; passenger; pilot; propeller; radio; wings; first; fast food restaurant; why?; because; castle; melt; paper; plasticine; wax; wood; make (something) from (...); too (near the sun); back; seat; appear; a hole; inventor; middle; piece; round; tyre; wheel; windmill. France. Spain; volcano, mobile phone; sports centre; tennis racket; Icarus; brothers; hours; seconds; dates; so (...); flight; mirror; a long time ago; explosion; suddenly; steal; wh-questions; each; by bike; by train; river;

beach; clock; dinosaur; east; engine; farmer; mountain; worker; around (you); carts; clever; collage. Mesopotamia; solid.
Sentences: who invented (...)?; they had (...); yes, they did/no, they didn't; sleep well. Keep fit.

A GIRAFFE WITHOUT SPOTS

Descriptions, plans: going to, Christmas,
town and city)

These are giraffes. This giraffe is very worried because she hasn't got spots.

'It doesn't mean,' says her mother. 'You are beautiful in this way.'

'No, Mum. I'm ridiculous. Everybody has got spots, but I haven't got them.'

'What are you going to do?' asks Mum.

'I'm going to buy artificial stickers...'

'Artificial spots are too expensive to buy…'

The young giraffe was desperate.

It was Christmas. She got a Christmas present: some artificial spots to stick.

The little giraffe
Is very sad,
It's Christmas Day
And Father Christmas appears.

She must change artificial stickers every three days. They are too expensive. There is a problem.
'What are you going to do?'
'I'm going to paint spots.'
They paint spots with crayons but the giraffe's skin absorbs them.
They paint them with plastic paint. The spots don't go away but they hurt… Two weeks later she hasn't got spots.
'What are you going to do?'

Artificial stickers
Are too expensive,
It's a problem,
No paintings
Her skin absorbs them,
What is she going to do?

A new family of giraffes arrives: father, mother and two children. They are beautiful, elegant, and extraordinary; the best in the world. The young giraffe likes them. She notices they haven't got spots…
The young giraffe looks at herself in the mirror: she is beautiful.
'I am not going to paint spots on myself. I don't need them.'
After that, the giraffe is happy with her appearance.

A new family
Of giraffes
Are elegant,
Without spots,
She likes her appearance,
They are happy,
One, two, three.

A GIRAFFE WITHOUT SPOTS

The little giraffe
Is very sad,
It's Christmas Day
And Father Christmas appears.

Artificial stickers
Are too expensive,
It's a problem,
No paintings
Her skin absorbs them,
What is she going to do?

A new family
Of giraffes
Are elegant,
Without spots,
She likes her appearance,
They are happy,
One, two, three.

PLANS, GOING TO: USEFUL LANGUAGE

Verbs: going to…; match; score; win; have fun; invite; fight; forget; grow; hide; save; come; cry; pack; stay; take; celebrate.

Vocabulary: cup; champion; team; golf; art gallery; balloons; invitations; sunglasses; dead; good luck; winner; dress; jacket; jeans; jumper; shirt; T-shirt; top; tracksuit; trainers; high; hungry; goodbye; sleeping bag; suitcase; torches; walking shoes; event; festival; Scotland; Scottish; traditional; game; anyway; The next Olympics; drink; food; newspapers; party; food and drink; battle; safe, shoes; bags; bus; camera, present, sweets, trip; a place far away; castles; lakes, mountains, rivers; bagpipes; costume; Highland Games. Kilt. Military Tattoo. Traditions.

Sentences: Sentences with "going to"; do press-ups; climb ropes; jog; lift weights; what about (...)?; let's (...); make soup; do homework; get on (...); play games; watch the match. Have a shower. What are you going to do?
Let's have (...).

CHRISTMAS: USEFUL LANGUAGE

Verbs: shine; wrap; decorate; dip; cut out; mix; roll; celebrate.

Vocabulary: angel; birdseed; Christmas dinner; cracker; hang; honey; pine cone; sleigh bells; snowman; Christmas; night; present; reindeer; snow; star; tree; Christmas table; carols; cake; Christmas tree; bell; candle; joy; kitten; peace; scarf; star; stocking; bookmark; bracelet; breadcrumbs; chimney; coconut; cream cheese; delicious; doll; fridge; snowball; umbrella; yum; bird; card; chocolates; Christmas; cousin; grandma; king; present (n); Santa Claus; sing; scissors; tree; uncle; dad; Father Christmas; Mum; sing carols; teacher; The Three Kings; tradition; witch; each one; Long tabs on the side.

Sentences: decorate the tree; wrap the presents. Fix the name tags. Fold serviettes to a triangle shape.

THE MAGIC GOAT
(town, city, transport and street)

A child goes to the fair with his parents.
'Can I have an action figure?'
'Perhaps there are no action figures here,' says Dad.
'There are animals, cars, lorries, trains, teddy bears… What about a goat?' says Mum.
'I like console games too,' says the boy.
'No,' says Mum. 'They are too expensive to buy.'
'This goat is magic,' says the toyshop assistant.
'I don't think so,' says the boy.
Finally, the child chooses the goat.

What do you want?
Cars, lorries, animals
Or a magic goat
I don't think so.

He touches his goat head.
'I wish a magic console game to play all the games in the world.'
A magic genie appears:
'Are you sure?' asks a magic genie.
'Yes' says the boy. 'My parents wouldn't buy it because it's too expensive and my marks are too low.'
'Your parents have got important reasons.'
'They don't understand me.'
'OK. Here you are! But, it's bad for you…' says the genie.

I touch the goat head
A genie appears
I ask for console games
Here you are, he says.

At home, the child goes to his bedroom, he forgets everything and he plays and plays console games. He doesn't have dinner, he doesn't sleep, and he plays all the night intensively. Next day he doesn't play with friends, he has got something to do. His teacher punishes him because he doesn't do his homework and he is absent-minded.

Mum knows something is happening. She goes to his bedroom. She sits down on the magic goat. The genie comes.

'Can I help you?' says the genie.

'Oh! How are you, my dear?' says Mum.

'Can you see the genie, Mum? says the boy.

'Yes, I can. I understand your necessity of things, sweet,' says Mum.

Playing console games
All day, all day,
He is absent-minded.
Mum can see the genie,
What is happening?

'Are you going to punish me?' asks the child.
'I wouldn't punish you if you solve your problem.'
'You only have a wish, young man!' says the genie.
'I want to get rid of this game, please. I want to be happy with my parents, my friends, and my school, with everything…'
'It's the right option,' says the genie. 'Bye.'
'Bye, genie' says the boy and his mum.
Mum takes the boy in her arms. Dad comes in…
'What's the matter?' says Dad.
'The genie is gone,' says the boy.
'Genies don't exist,' says Dad.
'I think so,' says Mum.

No magic genie
No console games,
Parents, school
And playing with friends.
You are happy
One, two, three.

THE MAGIC GOAT

What do you want?
Cars, lorries, animals
Or a magic goat
I don't think so.

I touch the goat head
A genie appears
I ask for console games
Here you are, he says.

Playing console games
All day, all day,
He is absent-minded.
Mum can see the genie,
What is happening?

No magic genie
No console games,
Parents, school
And playing with friends.
You are happy
One, two, three.

TRANSPORT AND STREET: USEFUL LANGUAGE

Transport: by (bus); on (foot); airport; bus stop; underground.
Street: traffic light; double-decker bus; open-top bus; house; school; corner shop; non-stop traffic.
Verbs: present simple; can; present continuous (future); imperatives, explore.
Vocabulary: bridge; quicksand; stepping stones; amber; day; night; wet paint; transport; family, newspaper, corner shop; so short; the top; prepositions; tourist; all the way; non-stop traffic; huge; a lot of space inside; Ford engine; normal; route; special; Piccadilly Circus; Oxford Street; Marble Arch; Hyde Park.
Sentences: turn right/left; go straight; across/up; excuse me, where's (...), please?; Near/in (...). (...)'s (shirt).

TOWN AND CITY, SHOPS: USEFUL LANGUAGE

Vocabulary: classroom objects; numbers 1-100; family; uncle; aunt; cousin; grandma; café; chemist's; cinema; library; park; supermarket; video shop; big/small; town; plurals, addresses; cave; mountain; river; waterfall; beautiful; country; flowers; trees; bus; car; street; market; theatre; weekend; too; roads; everywhere; lots of; a talking tree; both; wait!; boat; buildings; fair; scary; game; takeaway; castles; cities; forests; lakes; maze; palaces; weekend.
Verbs: delete, reply, save (mobile phone).
Grammar: This/that/these/those; there's/there're; is/are there?; there isn't/there are not.
Sentences: where do you live?; I live at (...); (...) lives in (...); how much is/are (...)?; it's/they're (...); in a/on a (...); do you like (...)?; what do you like?; where do you live?; I like (...); what's your telephone (mobile) number? It's (...);; Oh dear, poor you! What about (...)?

THE TELESCOPE WANTS TO BE ORIGINAL
(journeys, Valentine's Day)

It was Saint Valentine's Day. Dad came from a long journey. There are presents for everybody: a necklace for Mum, a wristwatch, for Dad; and a telescope for the boy. He likes astronomy.
The telescope wants to be original and different. In the beginning it works well but when it works for a long time, it changes its lens.

Happy Saint Valentine,
For all the family
A wristwatch for Dad,
A necklace for Mum
And a telescope for me.
It wants to be original
One, two, three.

wristwatch

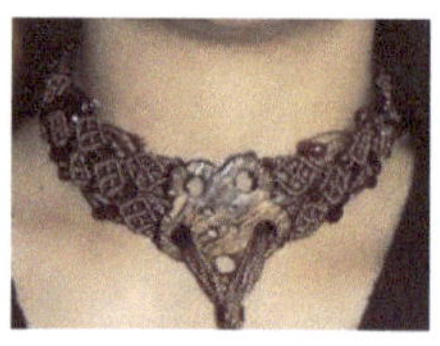

necklace

telescope

types of lens

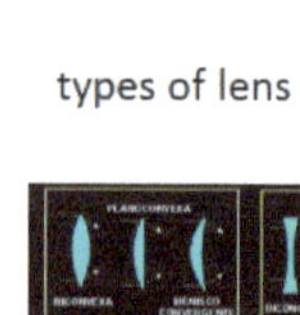

So, if the child wants to watch stars closely, he watches stars from a long way off. If the child wants to watch stars from a long way off, he watches stars closely…
The first day, it is amusing.
'What a strange thing!'
The second day the child is annoyed.
'This telescope doesn't work!'
The third day, the child is angry. He leaves the telescope.
'It's enough! I don't need you anymore.'
The child puts the telescope in a box. He puts the box in a cupboard. He takes the binoculars. He can't watch stars but he can watch something…

It doesn't work,
The child is angry,
Put it in a box,
Take the binoculars
And watch something.

from a long way

closely

the telescope doesn't work

binoculars

Once, the child wants to watch an eclipse. He needs the telescope to watch it.
'I'll give you a new opportunity!' says the child.
The telescope is bored in the box. It works correctly. The child likes it and he takes the telescope for ever.
You can be original but only a bit. Your originality can disturb other people.

I like your originality,
But only a bit,
Don't disturb me,
And I'll give you an opportunity.

from a long way

closely

binoculars

THE TELESCOPE WANTS TO BE ORIGINAL

Happy Saint Valentine,
For all the family
A wristwatch for Dad,
A necklace for Mum
And a telescope for me.
It wants to be original
One, two, three.

It doesn't work,
The child is angry,
Put it in a box,
Take the binoculars,
And watch something.

I like your originality,
But only a bit,
Don't disturb me,
And I'll give you an opportunity.

wristwatch

necklace

telescope

types of lens

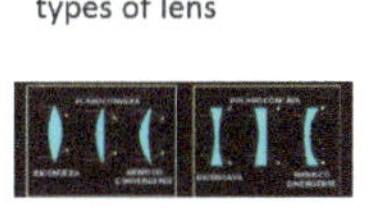

VALENTINE'S DAY: USEFUL LANGUAGE

Vocabulary: helpful; kind; Italy; message; rose; Saint Valentine; violet; heart; shape; beautiful; celebration, people, pot, smile, wonderful. 300 BC; feast day; goddess of marriage; idea; Juno; Roman; breakfast; cheese; delicious; flag; friend; mountain; neighbour; star; toast; Valentine; attach; between; felt tip pens; flap (n); glue; grill; lines; mobile card; out; piece; scissors; short; thread; trace; until.

Verbs: cut, fold, point.

JOURNEY: USEFUL LANGUAGE

Verbs: get rich; press; separate; explore; explorer; going to; imperatives; say; smile; past simple; present simple; need; move; enjoy; discover.

Vocabulary: excited; a hike; souvenirs; diving mask; hiking boots; money belt; suntan; writing postcards; bowl; camel; fried; jar; liquid; lump; pour; Egypt; Egyptian; pyramid; travellers; art; camera; cheese; maths; sunglasses; on holiday; in school; beach; bridge; cap; restaurant; torch; classroom objects; days of the week; flat (n); flower shop; job; treasure; crew; gift; first; next; then; finally; journey; neck; up/down; food; impossible; man in the moon; recipe; satellite dish; superlatives; activities and sports; city and places; jobs; countries; clothes; weather; north; south; east; west; high speed; the past; traveller; comparatives.

Sentences: dive off rocks; miss the bus; try different food; oh, no!; oh, good!; climb a mountain; keep a diary; visit monuments; turn right; transports and ways to travel; pack your bag; (...) just wanted.

USEFUL LANGUAGE FOR THE CLASSROOM

INTRODUCE YOURSELF: USEFUL LANGUAGE

Introduce yourself: Hello! I'm (...); what's your name?; his/her name's (...); I like your (...); how old are you?; I'm (ten); have you got (any brothers or sisters)?; I've got (...); I haven't got (...); animals. It's good to hear you. Let's all meet again. How old is he/she? What's his/her name? My/His / Her name is (...). Has he/she got a brother/sister? Where does he/she live? I like playing (the drums/English).He/She likes (playing guitar). She's good at (singing). I've/She's got a (...). He / She hasn't got a (...)? I have/No I haven't. Where/What does he sleep/eat? He sleeps (...)/eats (...).

Vocabulary: days of the week, objects of the classroom, the alphabet; age, family, food, everybody, great, rollerblades, twins, tennis racket, wardrobe, basket, summer camp, furniture, routines, animals and food; Open Day; welcome; days of the week, months and subjects; classroom; armchair, sock and shoe.

Sentences: where's/re my (pen/s)? Have got (objects / family); new; excuse me; here you are; please; sorry; thank you; thanks; my favourite (...) is (...); both. Hip, hip, hurray! This is (...).That's right. This is a (...). It's for (...). Something to (...). Beginning with (...). I love (...). (It) was. Sorry! Is it behind/in/on/under the table / door. Yes it is/No it isn't.

PRESENT SIMPLE AND PRESENT CONTINUOUS: USEFUL LANGUAGE

Verbs: Present Simple, Present Continuous. Past simple of verb to be; can; throw.

Vocabulary: dragon; knight/s; hero/es; kite; scared; parts of the body; legend; programme; kinds of stories (animal, adventure, true, funny); telling the time; plural of substantives; days of the week; hydra; cage; cave; comparatives; heroine; queen; Egypt; Greece; adjectives; animals; food, free time activities, sports, health, months of the year, ancient; message; crying; happy; laughing; sad; colours; the alphabet; action verbs; snorkelling; climbing; flying a kite; badminton; basketball; disco dancing; Atlantean fish; fantastic; fixing (things); language; machine; bright; here; too; very; hero / heroine; really; all; universe; hall; rock; cover; places; title; fight; sword; the bottom; coin; heads; tails; faces; faraway; handsome; arrows; art gallery, deer; lions; long ago; museum; painting; peasant: dream; love; piece (of cheese); everyday things; people to know; ; times long ago.

Sentences: do you like (adventure stories)? Yes, I do /No, I don't; there is/are; where was he from? has got; is good at; what's your favourite (...)?; where are you?; what are you doing?; I like/I don't like; free time activities and hobbies; what are you good at?; I'm good at (...);what you do/don't you like doing?; what about (...)?;listening to music; yes, I do/no, I don't; tickets; have you got (...)?; do you like (...)?; are/is (...)?; do you want to come? It doesn't work. Milo pushes the light. This is the wall. I can hear a voice. I've got a medal. I'm an artist. I think (...) is fantastic; breaking the door. Life was hard.

Computer vocabulary: browse; click; download; keyboard; Internet; mouse; screen; scroll down; magazine; newspaper; webpage; website.

SUBJECTS, DAYS OF THE WEEK, MONTHS: USEFUL LANGUAGE

Subjects, days and time: We have (Maths) on (Monday) at (3 o'clock); a quarter past/to; Art; Computer Studies;

English; Geography; History; Maths; Music; Science; Sport; my favourite subject is (...); What time do you (...)?; Africa;;
Vocabulary: timetable; days of the week, the time, friends; in the (morning); classroom; corridor; dining room; field; games; songs. Hurry!; marathon; quick; floors; ship; socks; hairy; scary; smiles; canoes; count: every day; history.
Verbs: clean; get dressed; wake up;   Present Simple; routines, get the bus; dreams; go to bed; have breakfast; clean my teeth; comb my hair; look in the mirror; learn, walk; the bottom of the ship.
Sentences: Let's go; there's; we have; I need (...); It's late. It's dark. Go away! Wait! Make things. Remember things.

ANIMALS / FOOD / COUNTRIES: USEFUL LANGUAGE

Animals: bison; chimpanzee; hippo; owl; parrot; zebra; brown bears; giant pandas; polar bears.
Food: berries, bamboo shoots; leaves, plants;
Sentences, wh- questions: What do they eat? They eat… Where are they from? they are from… Where do they live? They live in… They can (can/have got/are...); fly; jump; swing; angry.
Continents and countries: Africa; America; Poland; China
Places: cave; den; nest.
Bugs: ant; bee; beetle; bug; files; grasshopper; fly.

DESCRIPTIONS / COMPARATIVE AND SUPERLATIVE: USEFUL LANGUAGE

Adjectives: fat; thin; dark; fair; huge; short; tall; cold; hot; old; young; good looking; ugly; long; straight; curly; dark; fair; loud; beautiful;
Comparative and superlative: is (her sister) younger than (my sister)?; yes, she is; no, she isn't; (...);(...) is (...) than (...); the same as; is (...) (...) than (...)?; cheapest; more

expensive; smallest; biggest; good; better; best; slowest; fastest; bad; worse; worst.

Vocabulary: rat; tail; birthday; celebrate; illness; days of the week; months of the year; parts of the body; animals and parts of their body; llama; circle; line; same; smile; trousers; members of the family; cool! Invitation, show, emperor, face; around, down; magician, illusion; together, glasses; flute; piano; coffee; drum; violin; pop; rock; classical; guitarist; suitcase; prize; Broadway; front; musical; show (n); theatre, CD, guitar, ticket, t-shirt; monument, mountain, ocean, river, Oklahoma; the sound of music; the ground floor. XL (Extra Large), window, Hawaii, outside, youth festival.

Sentences: when's your birthday?; it's in… I can't wait. Right? Yuck! We're strong and fit. What are you talking about? Guess who. I know. Our eyes are playing tricks on our brains. What's happening? How much? Which?

Verbs: belongs to; relax; dance; study; explore; compose; Present Continuous. Past Simple. Can, break, maybe, put on (a musical), take, move, remember.

EASTER: USEFUL LANGUAGE

Vocabulary: champion; chicks; Easter; eggs; first; last; paint; American; behind; between; chocolate; garden; grass; many; stay; tree; colours; months of the year; kitten; lamb; piglet; puppy; fingerprints; need; pond; basket; field; football; sweets; animals; classroom objects; colours; cross the line; Easter Egg Roll; icing sugar; shape; symbol; huge; pond.

JOBS / PRESENT TO BE / WANT TO: USEFUL LANGUAGE

Jobs: cleaner; cook; dancer; dentist; photographer; pilot; reporter; singer; secretary; train driver.

Countries: Brazil; China; Ecuador; Spain; Italy; England; Great Britain; France; American; Brazilian; Chinese; English; French; Italian; Spanish.

Verbs: I want; he/she wants to be a (...); travel; present simple, 3rd person singular.

Vocabulary: film; uniform; the world; old languages; rocks; soil; study; mechanic; geologist; kitchen; an office; wonderful; guitar; night; paper; phone; shower; window; ambulance driver; flag; Red Cross; town; vet; village; never mind, smile, neighbours, city museum, collection, name, real, suddenly, team, hospital, night, people, school, weekends, lonely, mistery, crisis, emergency, organization.

Sentences: he/she's from (...). What does he/she do? He/she's a (...). Be careful. Yes, of course. Where's he from? All alone.

BIRTHDAY

Verbs: blow; invite, make a wish, cover, enjoy a treat.

Vocabulary: candle; present; special; balloon; bingo; invitation; moths of the year, festivals, bag, coloured sweets, jar of chocolate spread, packet.

HEALTH: USEFUL LANGUAGE

Sentences: What's the matter?; I've got a (cold / cough / headhache / sore throat / flu); I'm not very well; he's got a broken (...);; I can see (...); I'm red and hot. All day. Oh, dear! Follow me. Can you help me? Yes, of course. Yes, sure.

Verbs: imperatives; have got; can/can't; get well; there's/there're; celebrate; want; come; give a drink.
Vocabulary: earache; toothache; I'm better; baby; doctor; grandad; parts of the body; children; feet; teeth; drink; idea; sheep; a/an; lemon; honey; aliments; healthy; vet; wing, clown; funny; ill; joke; laughing; picnic; illness; nurse; except; every, roar, worried, box, down. Wow!; hospital, patients.

EARTH DAY: USEFUL LANGUAGE

Sentences: clean the water; Earth Day; plant more trees; recycle; save our planet; build bird houses; organise a nature walk; pick up rubbish; turn off the lights; please save.
Verbs: throw; wash; celebrate; help; let's; join; plant; save; want to.
Vocabulary: bin; a cake stall; cup; glass; bottle; by bike; planet; trees; earth-friendly.

WAS, WERE / DESCRIPTIONS: USEFUL LANGUAGE

Verbs: past simple of to be.
Vocabulary: claws; a vegetarian; comparative adjectives, appearance, parts of the body , sharp; numbers 1-100; friendly; scared; behind; forest; across; between; down; through; up; on; in; teddy; yesterday; peaceful; planet; spots; webbed; stairs, well; puppy; brain.
Sentences: How long was its body/were its claws? It was (...) metres long. How tall was it? How do you know that? Do you know this dinosaur? Follow the footsteps.

FOOD / IMPERATIVE: USEFUL LANGUAGE

Verbs: imperatives, present simple.
Food: mussels; oil; prawns; pepper; rice; red pepper; salt; vinegar; cereal; cheese; eggs; fruit; milk; tea; toast; yoghurt; black olives; boiled eggs; cooked potatoes; fizzy drink; mayonnaise; onion; peas; tomato; vegetables; across.

Vocabulary: fridge box; jug; pan; spoon; healthy; bug; first; later; llama; menu; next; palace; pie; restaurant; then; waitress; wife; add; cut; dish; mix; spoonful; strips; finally; diagonally; square; never mind; alarm clock; butter; clean your teeth; flavour; plum; biscuits; lettuce; score card; a criss-cross pattern; a treat; bedroom; kitchen; early; stretch; vegetarian; summer; winter; chocolate; ice; lemon; strawberry; adults; a long time; calcium; dessert; idea; metal bowl; protein; vitamin; special meal of the day.
Sentences: relax for a time. Call the waitress on the table. I've got an idea. Count the ticks. Go round three times. Put a counter on start. Throw the dice. Eat/sleep.

THERE WAS / THERE WERE: USEFUL LANGUAGE

Verbs: There was/were; past simple to be and regular verbs; erupt; present continuous; sail; build; change (v); conserve.
Prepositions: on/in/into; jump in/into; stand next to.
Vocabulary: pets' corner; playground; pond; see-saw; slide; swings; in 2001; hot; cold; rain; wind; a drought; a freeze; a flood; a hurricane; cloudy; dry; sunny; wet; windy; fireball; island; lake; the sea; the valley; crash into; destroy; sorry; alive; ash; thunderbolts; lucky; noise; scared; storm; strange; terrible; volcano; AD; August 24th; boats; fun; goat; horrid; hungry; the oceans; pelican; plants; sailor; the Eden Project; empty (v); greenhouse; machines; medicine; plants; plural nouns; park; shopping; pets; cities; forest; horses; Internet cafés; shops; days of the week; seasons; adjectives; dinosaur; lemur; diary; Italy; Naples; eggs; the land; rat; the sky; tortoise; lonesome; a future; a past; long ago; more and more; the last of my family; dates; planet; an enormous hole; Ever again; Impossible to work.
Sentences: (that) wasn't; do you remember (...)? Remember? What a shame! Everything is changing. Life (is good). Watch out. Live our lives the way they were before?

PAST SIMPLE: USEFUL LANGUAGE

Verbs: fly, flew; sail, sailed; erupt, erupted; rain, rained; change, changed; invent, invented, pull, pulled; change, changed the world.

Vocabulary: aeroplane; engine; kite; passenger; pilot; propeller; radio; wings; first; fast food restaurant; why?; because; castle; melt; paper; plasticine; wax; wood; make (something) from (...); too (near the sun); back; seat; appear; a hole; inventor; middle; piece; round; tyre; wheel; windmill. France. Spain; volcano, mobile phone; sports centre; tennis racket; Icarus; brothers; hours; seconds; dates; so (...); flight; mirror; a long time ago; explosion; suddenly; steal; wh-questions; each; by bike; by train; river; beach; clock; dinosaur; east; engine; farmer; mountain; worker; around (you); carts; clever; collage. Mesopotamia; solid.

Sentences: who invented (...)?; they had (...); yes, they did/no, they didn't; sleep well. Keep fit.

PLANS, GOING TO: USEFUL LANGUAGE

Verbs: going to...; match; score; win; have fun; invite; fight; forget; grow; hide; save; come; cry; pack; stay; take; celebrate.

Vocabulary: cup; champion; team; golf; art gallery; balloons; invitations; sunglasses; dead; good luck; winner; dress; jacket; jeans; jumper; shirt; T-shirt; top; tracksuit; trainers; high; hungry; goodbye; sleeping bag; suitcase; torches; walking shoes; event; festival; Scotland; Scottish; traditional; game; anyway; The next Olympics; drink; food; newspapers; party; food and drink; battle; safe, shoes; bags; bus; camera, present, sweets, trip; a place far away; castles; lakes, mountains, rivers; bagpipes; costume; Highland Games. Kilt. Military Tattoo. Traditions.

Sentences: Sentences with "going to"; do press-ups; climb ropes; jog; lift weights; what about (...)?; let's (...); make soup; do homework; get on (...); play games; watch the match. Have a shower. What are you going to do?
Let's have (...).

CHRISTMAS: USEFUL LANGUAGE

Verbs: shine; wrap; decorate; dip; cut out; mix; roll; celebrate.

Vocabulary: angel; birdseed; Christmas dinner; cracker; hang; honey; pine cone; sleigh bells; snowman; Christmas; night; present; reindeer; snow; star; tree; Christmas table; carols; cake; Christmas tree; bell; candle; joy; kitten; peace; scarf; star; stocking; bookmark; bracelet; breadcrumbs; chimney; coconut; cream cheese; delicious; doll; fridge; snowball; umbrella; yum; bird; card; chocolates; Christmas; cousin; grandma; king; present (n); Santa Claus; sing; scissors; tree; uncle; dad; Father Christmas; Mum; sing carols; teacher; Befana; The Three Kings; tradition; witch; each one; Long tabs on the side.

Sentences: decorate the tree; wrap the presents. Fix the name tags. Fold serviettes to a triangle shape.

TRANSPORT AND STREET: USEFUL LANGUAGE

Transport: by (bus); on (foot); airport; bus stop; underground.

Street: traffic light; double-decker bus; open-top bus; house; school; corner shop; non-stop traffic.

Verbs: present simple; can; present continuous (future); imperatives, explore.

Vocabulary: bridge; quicksand; stepping stones; amber; day; night; wet paint; transport; family, newspaper, corner shop; so short; the top; prepositions; tourist; all the way; non-stop traffic; huge; a lot of space inside; Ford engine; normal; route; special; Piccadilly Circus; Oxford Street; Marble Arch; Hyde Park.

Sentences: turn right/left; go straight; across/up; excuse me, where's (...), please?; Near/in (...). (...)'s (shirt).

TOWN AND CITY, SHOPS: USEFUL LANGUAGE

Vocabulary: classroom objects; numbers 1-100; family; uncle; aunt; cousin; grandma; café; chemist's; cinema; library; park; supermarket; video shop; big/small; town; plurals, addresses; cave; mountain; river; waterfall; beautiful; country; flowers; trees; bus; car; street; market; theatre; weekend; too; roads; everywhere; lots of; a talking tree; both; wait!; boat; buildings; fair; scary; game; takeaway; castles; cities; forests; lakes; maze; palaces; weekend.
Verbs: delete, reply, save (mobile phone).
Grammar: This/that/these/those; there's/there're; is/are there?; there isn't/there are not.
Sentences: where do you live?; I live at (...); (...) lives in (...); how much is/are (...)?; it's/they're (...); in a/on a (...); do you like (...)?; what do you like?; where do you live?; I like (...); what's your telephone (mobile) number? It's (...);; Oh dear, poor you! What about (...)?

VALENTINE'S DAY: USEFUL LANGUAGE

Vocabulary: helpful; kind; Italy; message; rose; Saint Valentine; violet; heart; shape; beautiful; celebration, people, pot, smile, wonderful. 300 BC; feast day; goddess of marriage; idea; Juno; Roman; breakfast; cheese; delicious; flag; friend; mountain; neighbour; star; toast; Valentine; attach; between; felt tip pens; flap (n); glue; grill; lines; mobile card; out; piece; scissors; short; thread; trace; until.
Verbs: cut, fold, point.

JOURNEY: USEFUL LANGUAGE

Verbs: get rich; press; separate; explore; explorer; going to; imperatives; say; smile; past simple; present simple; need; move; enjoy; discover.

Vocabulary: excited; a hike; souvenirs; diving mask; hiking boots; money belt; suntan; writing postcards; bowl; camel; fried; jar; liquid; lump; pour; Egypt; Egyptian; pyramid; travellers; art; camera; cheese; maths; sunglasses; on holiday; in school; beach; bridge; cap; restaurant; torch; classroom objects; days of the week; flat (n); flower shop; job; treasure; crew; gift; first; next; then; finally; journey; neck; up/down; food; impossible; man in the moon; recipe; satellite dish; superlatives; activities and sports; city and places; jobs; countries; clothes; weather; north; south; east; west; high speed; the past; traveller; comparatives.

Sentences: dive off rocks; miss the bus; try different food; oh, no!; oh, good!; climb a mountain; keep a diary; visit monuments; turn right; transports and ways to travel; pack your bag; (...) just wanted.